OUT OF THIS WORLD!

Answers to Questions About Space

by Isabel Thomas

raintree

a Capstone company — publishers for children

Engage Literacy is published in the UK by Raintree.
Raintree is an imprint of Capstone Global Library Limited, a company incorporated in England and Wales having its registered office at 264 Banbury Road, Oxford, OX2 7DY – Registered company number: 6695582

www.raintree.co.uk

Editorial credits
Gina Kammer, editor; Peggie Carley and Cynthia Della-Rovere, designers; Kelly Garvin, media researcher; Katy LaVigne, production specialist

Image credits
NASA: ESA/Giotto Project, 29, ESA/Hubble & NASA, 31, John Hopkins University Applied Physics Laboratory, 15, JPL/John Hopkins University Applied Physics Laboratory/Southwest Research Institute, 18, JPL/Caltech, 41, JPL/Caltech/Malin Space Science Systems, 42, JPL/Caltech/MSSS, 21, JPL/ESA/ATG medialab, 19, JPL/ESA/Rosetta/VAVCAM, 28, JPL/SDO, 12, Lunar and Planetary Institute, 10-11, Sandy Joseph and Tim Terry, 27; Newscom/CHINE NOUVELLE/SIPA, 40; Science Source: 34, 38, Mark Garlick, 43, Pekka Parviainen, 45; Shutterstock: agsandrew, 37, Andrew F. Kazmierski, 46, Andrey Armyagov, 8, Denis Belitsky, 30, Designua, 6, Elenarts, cover (bl), 1 (t), fabiodevilla, 16-17 (background), Igor Zh., 13, janez volmajer, cover (t), 1 (b), John A. Davis, 7, Lucian, 25, Mirai, 22-23, Mopic, cover (br), 14, oorka, 20, peresanz, 44, photomaster, 9, puchan, 25, pyty, 26, sciencepics, 16-17, studio23, 25, Tatyana Vyc, 32, Triff, cover (background), Vadim Sadovski, 25, vectortatu, 33, Yuriy Mazur, backcover, 5, Superstock/Hemls.fr, 4

Printed and bound in India.

Out of This World!: Answers to Questions About Space

ISBN: 978 1 4747 4660 1

CONTENTS

How much do you know about space?

Are you a space expert? Would you be able to spot the Pole Star in the night sky?

Humans have been studying the skies for thousands of years. They have recorded their findings on everything from cave walls to computers. Endless questions have led to amazing findings. But we don't know everything about space. Every year, new discoveries lead to even more questions!

An ancient star map was painted in a cave in France.

For scientists, no question is too strange. In fact, the strangest questions can lead to some of the most exciting answers. Are you ready to put your questions to the test and upgrade your space knowledge from earthly to out of this world?

QUICK QUIZ

The quiz at the end of each chapter will test your growing knowledge of space. Refer back to the text to find the answers. The key is on page 48.

The Earth and Moon

Let's begin close to home. How far away is space from us? The Moon and some planets are the closest to Earth, but they are still far out in space.

Where does space begin?

It's easy to think that space begins where Earth's *atmosphere* stops, but it's not that simple. The air gets thinner and thinner the higher you go, and there is no hard line. After asking the question for years, most scientists now agree that space starts at the *Kármán Line*. This is a made-up line 100 kilometres above Earth's surface. In most countries, you have to cross the Kármán Line to become an astronaut. In the United States, astronauts can earn their wings by flying 80 kilometres above the surface.

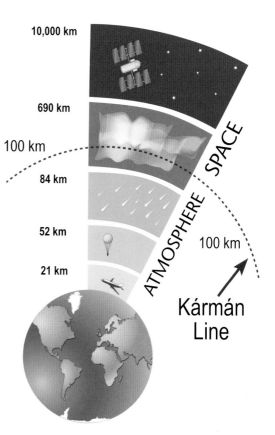

10,000 km

690 km

100 km

84 km

52 km

21 km

ATMOSPHERE   SPACE

100 km

Kármán
Line

100 kilometres isn't far – why isn't everyone an astronaut?

Gravity makes it difficult to become an astronaut. It is a force that pulls objects together. The bigger the object, the stronger its gravity. This is why you fall back towards Earth when you leap up rather than stay in the air. To escape the pull of Earth's gravity, you need a big push in the opposite direction. This pushing force often comes from rockets. These are so costly to build and launch into space that fewer than 600 people have been into space.

Push of rocket

Pull of gravity

The space shuttle Atlantis used more than 2 million litres of fuel to beat gravity!

What have we sent into space?

Most objects that humans send into space don't escape Earth's gravity. They go into *orbit*, travelling around the planet. Thousands of these human-made *satellites* orbit our planet. They help people send messages or get directions. They also send data about the weather back to Earth. Because they are orbiting above the Kármán line, we say they are in space.

More than 1,400 working satellites are in orbit. This doesn't include the thousands in orbit that no longer work!

Why does the Moon seem to change shape?

The Moon is a natural satellite held by Earth's gravity. It is a huge ball of rock that orbits Earth. It doesn't produce its own light. So from Earth we can only see the half of the Moon that is lit up by the Sun. As the Moon orbits Earth our view changes, and we see different amounts of the sunny side. This makes it look as if the Moon is changing shape!

Why does the Moon look patchy?

The ancient Greeks thought the dark spots on the Moon were water. On the first maps of the Moon, they were given water names such as the Marsh of Decay. Since then, telescopes, human explorers and space *probes* have shown that there is no liquid water on the Moon. The dark spots are cooled lava that may have flowed on the surface billions of years ago. These flat areas, called "plains", reflect less sunlight than the mountains that surround them, so they look darker from Earth.

Why do we always see the same side of the Moon?

A full Moon always looks the same. As it orbits Earth, the Moon also turns very slowly on its *axis*. The spin and orbit move at the same time, so that the same side of the Moon will always face towards Earth.

What's on the far side of the Moon?

Scientists wanted to know about the far side of the Moon, so they sent a space probe, Luna 3, to take pictures of it in 1959. The far side doesn't look like our view. There are fewer plains, and the mountain regions are about 5 kilometres higher. There are also more *craters*.

Luna 3 was sent into space by the former Soviet Union. Many of the regions on the far side of the Moon are named after Soviet people and places.

Far side of the Moon

plains

mountains

crater

QUICK QUIZ

Test your knowledge before moving out of orbit.

To become an astronaut you have to
a) buy a spacesuit
b) cross the 80 kilometre line
c) go into orbit.

THE SUN

As the Moon orbits Earth, our planet is also in orbit around a much bigger object – the Sun. How much do you know about the star in our Solar System?

What is the Sun made of?

Like all stars the Sun is a ball of hot, glowing gases. At the centre of this ball, the *pressure* and temperature are so high that *particles* are pushed together until they combine. This gives off huge amounts of energy. Some of it escapes into space as *radiation* in the form of light and heat.

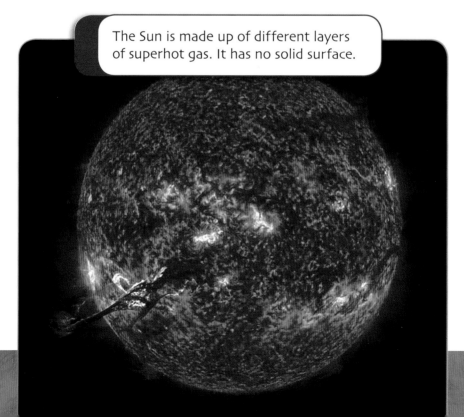

The Sun is made up of different layers of superhot gas. It has no solid surface.

solar eclipse

From Earth, the Sun and Moon look the same size. This is why the Moon can block the light of the Sun in a solar eclipse.

How big is the Sun?

The Sun is enormous! At its widest part, the Sun is 1.4 million kilometres across. This is wide enough to line up 109 Earths side by side. Compared with other stars, the Sun is only medium-sized.

Why do the Sun and Moon look the same size from Earth?

Although the Sun is 400 times wider than the Moon, it is also about 400 times further away. This means that the Sun and Moon look the same size from Earth.

How close could a spaceship get to the Sun?

The temperature at the Sun's core, or centre, is about 15 million degrees Celsius. The surface is about 5,500 degrees Celsius, which is hot enough to boil most things found on Earth. A spaceship would not be able to reach the surface because the *corona*, or outer layer, of the Sun's atmosphere is even hotter! Solar Probe Plus will be the first space probe to fly into the Sun's corona. It will get as close as 6.3 million kilometres to the Sun. It will do this using a heat shield that can cope with high temperatures.

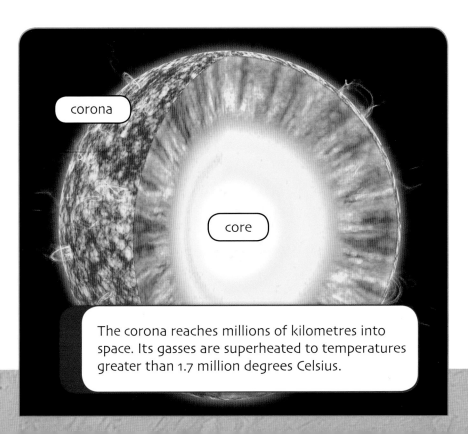

corona

core

The corona reaches millions of kilometres into space. Its gasses are superheated to temperatures greater than 1.7 million degrees Celsius.

Solar Probe Plus will find out more about the energy released by the Sun and how it affects Earth.

How long would it take to get to the Sun?

The Sun is about 150 million kilometres from Earth. This is a short distance if you are moving at the speed of light. The speed of light is the rate at which light moves. Light from the Sun's surface reaches Earth in about eight minutes. Humans can't travel at the speed of light. Solar Probe Plus will travel at up to 720,000 kilometres per hour. That's fast enough to get from London, England, to New York City in the United States in less than 30 seconds. But the route the probe will fly to go deeper into the Sun's atmosphere means that the trip will take more than six years.

Will the Sun shine forever?

Stars don't shine forever. As the Sun's supply of fuel runs out, in about 5 billion years, it will become brighter and get bigger. Stars like this are known as red giants. As its outer layers of gas begin to escape into space, the Sun will shrink and become a white dwarf star. Dwarf stars are about the size of a planet. The white dwarf will slowly cool down until it stops shining. It will become a black dwarf, which can hardly be seen in space.

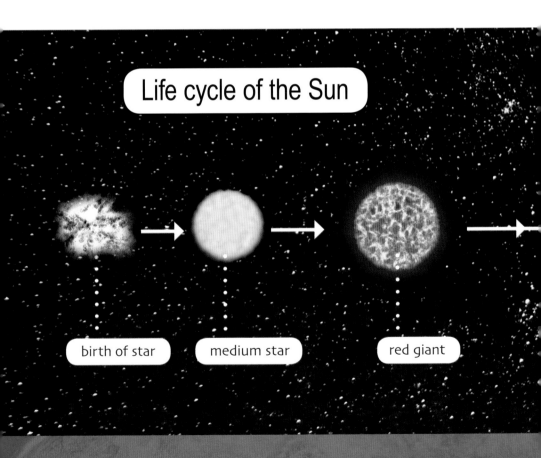

Life cycle of the Sun

birth of star   medium star   red giant

QUICK QUIZ

Are you ready to explore the rest of the solar system?

How long does it take for light leaving the Sun's surface to reach Earth?

a) eight minutes
b) one light year
c) six years

The Sun began with enough fuel to last about 10 billion years. It is about halfway through its life.

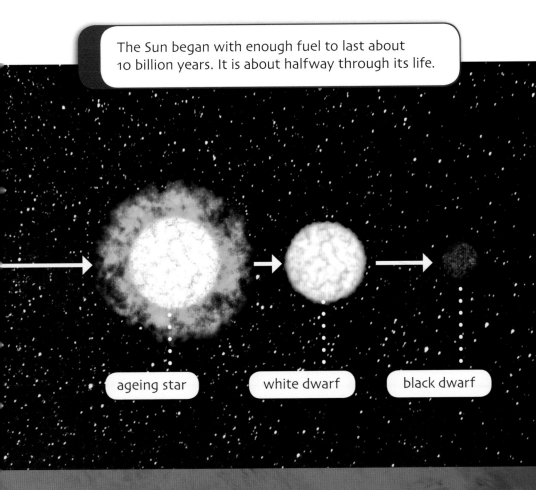

ageing star   white dwarf   black dwarf

Planets and moons

Let's find out more about our nearest neighbours – the other planets and moons in our solar system.

What is a planet?

Isn't a planet a huge, ball-shaped object that orbits the Sun? Like most things in space, it's not that simple. The list of planets in our solar system has changed several times in the last 150 years. Scientists believed there were nine planets until 2006. Today they say that planets must have gravity strong enough to pull in any other large objects or push them back out of their path. There are eight planets in our solar system that fit this rule.

Charon

Pluto is only about twice as big as one of its moons, Charon.

Pluto

What happened to the ninth planet?

Pluto, the ninth planet, is still there – but it was moved down a class. Pluto was listed as a planet until 2006, when it was decided that it was a *dwarf planet* after all. Dwarf planets are mostly round, but unlike planets their gravity is not as strong. This means that dwarf planets share their path around the Sun with smaller objects. These objects include *asteroids* or the icy rocks of the Kuiper Belt. The Kuiper Belt is similar to the asteroid belt, but it is further from the Sun. The first five dwarf planets found in our solar system were Ceres, Pluto, Haumea, Makemake and Eris. Other dwarf planets have also been spotted in the Kuiper Belt.

How do the eight planets compare?

The four planets closest to the Sun are small and rocky. Like Earth, the planets Mercury, Venus and Mars have solid surfaces you could land on. Conditions on these planets are not like on Earth. Venus and Mars have atmospheres that would poison living things. Tiny Mercury barely has an atmosphere at all. The other four planets in the solar system are known as the gas giants – Jupiter, Saturn, Uranus and Neptune. They are far bigger than the rocky planets.

Comparing the sizes of the eight planets

Some planets are small when compared to other planets. But large or small, they are all planets because of their gravity!

Which planet is most like home?

Venus is almost the same size as Earth and has been called our planet's twin. Yet, it would be deadly to set foot on this planet. Its thick atmosphere acts like a greenhouse. It traps the Sun's heat and makes Venus the hottest planet in the solar system. Mars is about half the size of Earth and cooler because it is further from the Sun. Like Earth, it has polar ice caps. There are plenty of signs that there were once oceans, lakes and flowing rivers on Mars. The water is now hidden beneath the surface but sometimes still seeps through.

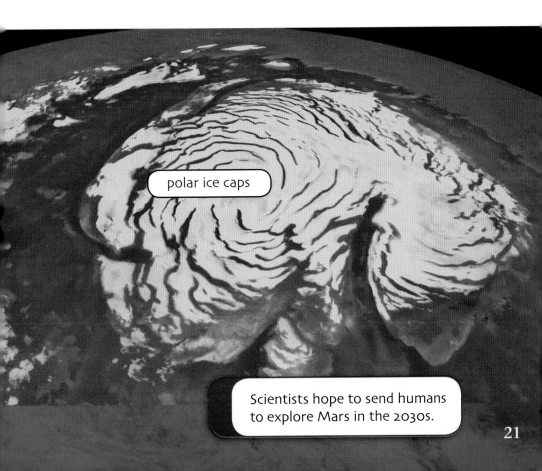

polar ice caps

Scientists hope to send humans to explore Mars in the 2030s.

Are other moons like our Moon?

All the planets have moons except for Mercury and Venus. The gas giants Jupiter and Saturn have more than 60 moons each! Many of these seem to be more exciting places than our Moon, and scientists are eager to find out more. One of Jupiter's moons, Europa, seems to have twice as much water as Earth. Perhaps there is life below its icy crust. One of Saturn's moons, Titan, is bigger than Mercury and has a thick atmosphere like Earth's.

Scientists believe Jupiter has up to 67 moons. Fourteen of them haven't been named yet.

QUICK QUIZ

Is your brain as big as a planet, yet?

Which of these planets is a gas giant?

a) Earth   b) Venus   c) Neptune

Asteroids, comets and meteorites

There are billions of other rocks flying around our solar system.

What is the asteroid belt?

The asteroid belt is a region of space between Mars and Jupiter. It's full of orbiting rubble, left over from when the solar system was forming. Sometimes one of these space rocks, or asteroids, is nudged out of the belt and goes zooming towards the Sun. A small lump of rock that's moving through space but is smaller than an asteroid is known as a *meteoroid.*

What happens if a meteoroid collides with Earth?

Meteoroids collide with Earth millions of times every day. When one enters Earth's atmosphere, it rubs against the air. This *friction* causes the rock to heat up. It becomes so hot that it glows.

These glowing space rocks are known as shooting stars, but scientists call them *meteors.* Most boil away to nothing. But those that are larger than 30 kilograms often make it to the ground! Then they are known as *meteorites.*

Could a meteorite land in my garden?

Meteorites could land in your garden, but most of them are tiny. Some of the dust in your garden comes from outer space, but it won't leave craters on your lawn. That's a good thing. Large meteorites make craters about 20 times bigger around than they are!

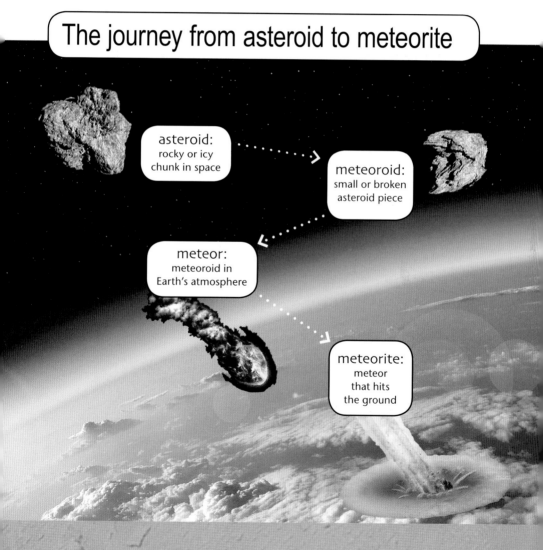

The journey from asteroid to meteorite

asteroid:
rocky or icy
chunk in space

meteoroid:
small or broken
asteroid piece

meteor:
meteoroid in
Earth's atmosphere

meteorite:
meteor
that hits
the ground

What if a large asteroid hit Earth?

An asteroid big enough to do major damage hits Earth once around every 2,000 years. The asteroid Eros' orbit brings it close to Earth – in 2012, it was just over 26 million kilometres away. This is about 70 times further than the Moon. Eros has a 5 per cent chance of hitting Earth in the next million years!

How worried should we be?

Scientists track more than 1,700 large asteroids. They are bigger than 140 metres across and have orbits that come close to crossing Earth's orbit. There is a chance they could collide with Earth in the future, but it doesn't mean that they will.

The Hoba West meteorite in Namibia is the largest found on Earth. It is 2.7 metres across.

Could we land on an asteroid?

Asteroids are rich in metals, such as iron and nickel, which would be useful on Earth. Space probes have already landed on an asteroid and a comet. The next step is finding out how to get rocks back to Earth. NASA's OSIRIS-REx Mission will visit the asteroid Bennu. The spacecraft has no people on board. It will use a machine to grab a sample of rock to bring back to Earth.

The OSIRIS-REx will spend two years orbiting the asteroid Bennu.

Why do comets have tails?

Comets don't have tails until they get close to the Sun. There are billions of icy comets in the outer solar system, but they are too small to see. When a comet nears the inner solar system, it becomes much brighter. Its icy surface melts and boils, and a long tail of *vapour* forms. No matter which direction the comet is moving in, the tail always points away from the Sun.

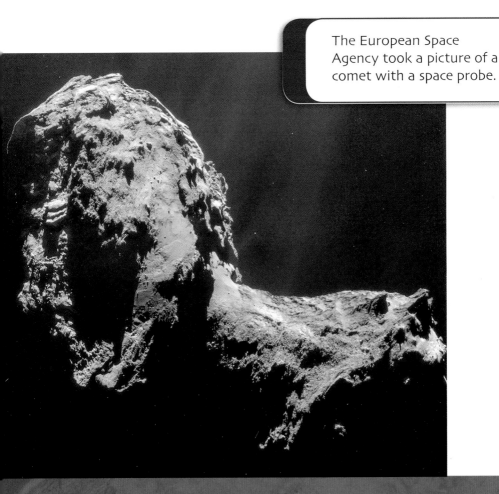

The European Space Agency took a picture of a comet with a space probe.

comet's tail

The tail of a comet can stretch for millions of kilometres across space.

QUICK QUIZ

Test your space rock knowledge before moving out of our solar system.

What is a meteorite?

a) a lump of rock in the asteroid belt

b) a space rock speeding through Earth's atmosphere

c) a space rock that has landed on Earth

GALAXIES AND STARS

A galaxy is a group of stars, gas and dust held together by gravity. Let's start by looking at our own galaxy – the Milky Way.

How many stars are in a galaxy?

The Sun is one of at least 100 billion stars in the Milky Way. Many of these stars are bunched together towards the centre of the galaxy. The Milky Way is huge – even light takes 100,000 years to cross it. But in galaxy terms it is just medium-sized. The largest one ever spotted is called IC 1101 and has up to 100 trillion stars. It is more than 50 times the size of the Milky Way.

The centre of our own galaxy is a cluster of at least 500 million stars. It is one of the brightest things we can see in the night sky.

Can we visit the other stars in our galaxy?

Our nearest star apart from the Sun is called Proxima Centauri. At more than 40 trillion kilometres away, even our fastest spacecraft would take thousands of years to get there.

Proxima Centauri

Proxima Centauri is a fairly small, dim star. We can't see it in the night sky without a very powerful telescope.

What is a constellation?

From here, stars look like dots of light around Earth. We might think that these dots are all the same distance from Earth. We join them to create shapes called constellations. But really, space is *three-dimensional*, having length, width and depth. Some stars in a constellation are much further from Earth than others. But they are still useful tools. They help astronomers to divide the vast sky up into 88 regions. Doing so is helpful for pointing others who study space in the right direction.

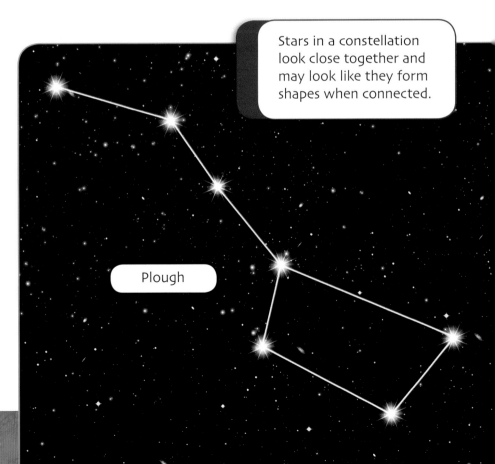

Stars in a constellation look close together and may look like they form shapes when connected.

Plough

Are all galaxies spiral shaped?

About two-thirds of galaxies have a spiral shape. The Milky Way is one of these. Others fall into three other groups. Lenticular galaxies are shaped like the lens in a magnifying glass. Elliptical galaxies are oval, like an egg. Irregular galaxies don't follow any of the other shapes.

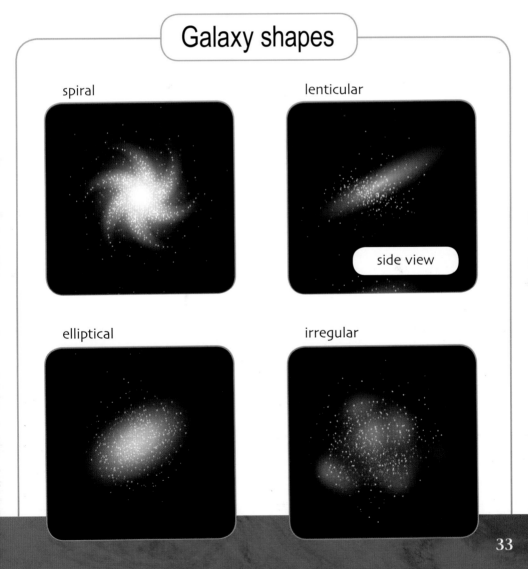

Galaxy shapes

spiral

lenticular

side view

elliptical

irregular

What's at the centre of a galaxy?

The galaxy's centre is a big *black hole*. Black holes are places in space that can't be seen. Astronomers have found that a huge black hole is likely to lie at the centre of almost every galaxy. Each one weighs hundreds of millions times more than our Sun. This makes their gravity so strong that not even light can escape. And this means we can't see them. The largest black holes keep growing as they gobble up dust and gas from nearby stars. As all this dust and gas falls into the black hole, the region around it heats up and gives off energy.

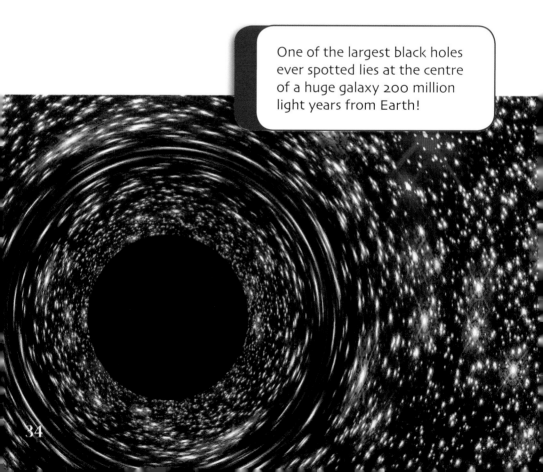

One of the largest black holes ever spotted lies at the centre of a huge galaxy 200 million light years from Earth!

What happens when galaxies collide?

The part of the universe that we can see from Earth contains more than 2 trillion galaxies! They are always on the move. They often bend each other out of shape or even collide. This takes hundreds of millions of years. There is so much space between the stars in each galaxy that they rarely hit each other. Instead, they slowly merge to become one large galaxy.

Our own galaxy is running into another one right now. The crash began around 2 billion years ago. The small galaxy is slowly being torn apart and drawn towards the centre of the Milky Way. Scientists think this may have given the Milky Way its spiral arms. Another huge galaxy is also falling towards us – though it won't start to affect the Milky Way for a few billion years.

QUICK QUIZ

Don't let a black hole gobble up the right answer!

What shape is the Milky Way?
a) ball-shaped
b) spiral-shaped
c) lens-shaped

THE UNIVERSE

It's a small page turn for your hand but a giant leap for your brain. Are you ready to explore the science of the universe?

How big is the universe?

The universe is big and getting bigger! We know the universe is expanding because distant galaxies are getting even further away. This means it must have been smaller in the past. And all the things in it were once closely packed together. This led some astronomers to the Big Bang theory. This is the idea that billions of years ago, a tiny, hot universe suddenly expanded. It created space, energy and *matter*. Matter is the particles that everything is made of.

What happened after the Big Bang?

In the Big Bang theory, the universe right after the Big Bang was nothing like the one we see today. It was a mixture of tiny particles, light and energy. As the mixture expanded and cooled, particles began clumping together to form the first stars and galaxies.

How old is the universe?

To work out how old the universe is, scientists have studied the "glow" they think is left over from the Big Bang. By finding out how long this glow has been cooling down, some scientists believe that the universe is 13.8 billion years old.

When stars explode, huge amounts of energy are released. Seeing these stars shows scientists that the universe is expanding faster and faster.

Why is astronomy like time travel?

When scientists look at a galaxy 4 billion light years away, they see it as it was 4 billion years ago. This is because the light has taken 4 billion years to reach Earth. They are looking back in time!

The parts of the universe that we can spot from Earth are known as the observable universe. The whole universe is likely to be much bigger than this.

Is the space between stars and galaxies empty?

To a human, the space between stars and galaxies looks empty. We can see no light, and there is no air to carry *sound waves*. So even a huge blast in space would be silent. But in fact much of the matter in the universe is not part of stars or planets. It is found between them as gas and dust.

Is there anything left to discover?

There is much more matter in the universe than we can see. Scientists know this "dark matter" must be there, because they can see the effect that its gravity has on galaxies. But they still don't know just what dark matter is. As this matter makes up around a quarter of the universe, they are very eager to find out.

QUICK QUIZ

Can you ride the waves of space yet?

Scientists think the universe is
a) getting bigger
b) getting smaller
c) staying the same.

Exploring space

On a very dark night, human eyes can see about 5,000 stars in the sky. Early astronomers found out a lot about space simply by tracking the movement of these stars across the night sky. But telescopes opened up the universe.

What can telescopes see that I can't?

The first telescopes were invented just over 400 years ago. They made distant space objects look much bigger and brighter. Astronomers could see hundreds of thousands of stars in the night sky. Over time, telescopes got bigger and better. New ones have been made to spot different kinds of radiation that we can't see with our eyes. They allowed us to detect cooler, fainter stars, distant galaxies and superhot regions such as black holes.

The world's largest radio telescope has been built in China. It can spot radio waves given out by distant objects in space.

Why can't we see these colours in the night sky?

As well as light, stars and galaxies give out many other types of radiation. False colours are added to pictures to show the types of energy that a star or galaxy is giving out. This helps astronomers to know that part of space better.

False colours were used in this image taken by a telescope. The colours show two regions where stars are forming in our galaxy.

The photographs sent back to Earth by a space probe or rover are much more detailed than photographs we can take using telescopes on Earth.

Why do we need to send spacecraft into space?

Scientists can find out a great deal about the universe using things such as telescopes on Earth. But think how hard it might be to learn about a forest from pictures alone. You can learn a great deal, but to really understand it and to see the details you need to visit. Space probes have gone to every planet in our solar system and have landed on many of them. Robot rovers have travelled across the surface of Mars, taking in data and samples. People have even visited the Moon in person, bringing back samples of Moon rock to Earth.

Where is the best place to look for life beyond Earth?

Scientists are on the lookout for "Goldilocks" planets. These planets orbit stars at a distance that makes them not too hot and not too cold for life. They spot these planets by looking for the dip in starlight that happens when a planet orbits in front of a star. There may also be tiny living things living elsewhere in our solar system. The most likely places to look are those moons and planets that have water.

Astronomers using a giant telescope have spotted an Earth-sized planet orbiting a star near the Sun. An artist has pictured a view from the planet – with two suns!

QUICK QUIZ

Get this right and you're well on your way to astronomer status!

A Goldilocks planet is
a) a planet that is just the right distance from a star
b) a planet that is home to aliens
c) a planet that has two suns.

Over and out

Hurray! Your brain is powered up with space knowledge. But don't take our word for it! Space starts 100 kilometres above your head. But it's easy to start exploring the universe from the comfort of Earth. Here are some things to try.

Stargazing

Try spotting some constellations from your garden. Download a star map. Stand away from lights. Give your eyes about 20 minutes to adjust to the dark – you'll be able to see many more stars.

Planet spotting

You can use constellations to help you locate the planets in our solar system. Mercury, Venus, Mars, Jupiter and Saturn can all be seen with the naked eye. But their places change throughout the year so you'll need a star chart to tell you where to look. Search for a free app to help you.

Binoculars

With a pair of binoculars, you can see an extra 200,000 stars and the rings around Saturn. Some amazing things have been found this way. Maybe you'll even make a discovery of your own.

The Hyakutake Comet was discovered by a person with a pair of binoculars!

Glossary

asteroid large rock that moves through space but is smaller than a planet

atmosphere layer of gases that surrounds some planets, dwarf planets and moons

axis real or imaginary line through the centre of an object, around which the object turns

black hole invisible region of space with strong gravity

corona outer layer of the Sun's atmosphere

crater large hole in the ground caused by crashing rocks

dwarf planet rocky ball that orbits the sun but has not cleared the orbit of neighbouring planets

friction force produced when two objects rub against each other

Kármán Line boundary or imaginary line that separates Earth from space

matter anything that has weight and takes up space

meteor chunk of metal or rock that enters Earth's atmosphere, causing a streak of light in the sky; also called a shooting star

meteorite chunk of an asteroid or comet that lands on Earth's surface

meteoroid rocky or metallic chunk of an asteroid travelling through space

microbe tiny living thing that is too small to be seen without a microscope

orbit path of one body around another

particle small piece of matter

pressure force that pushes on something

probe small vehicle used to explore objects in outer space

radiation tiny particles or waves of energy given off by something

satellite natural or human-made object in space that circles a larger object, such as a planet

sound wave wave or vibration that can be heard

three-dimensional having length, depth and height

vapour gas made from a liquid

Index

Quiz answers: 11b, 17a, 23c, 29c, 35b, 39a, 43a